CROCK·POT.

◆ THE ORIGINAL SLOW COOKER ◆

CHICKEN

Publications International, Ltd.

Pictured on the front cover: Indian-Style Apricot Chicken *(page 42).*
Pictured on the back cover (clockwise from top): Cashew Chicken *(page 64),* Moroccan-Spiced Chicken Wings *(page 8)* and Autumn Chicken *(page 60).*

ISBN-13: 978-1-4127-2939-0
ISBN-10: 1-4127-2939-4

Library of Congress Control Number: 2008924181

Manufactured in China.

8 7 6 5 4 3 2 1

TABLE OF CONTENTS

INTRODUCTION

Slow Cooking Hints and Tips

Slow Cooker Sizes

Smaller slow cookers, such as 1- to 3½-quart models, are the perfect size for singles, a couple, empty-nesters and for serving dips.

While medium-size slow cookers (those holding somewhere between 3 and 5 quarts) will easily cook enough food to feed a small family, they're also convenient for holiday side dishes and appetizers.

Large slow cookers are great for big family dinners, holiday entertaining, and potluck suppers. A 6- to 7-quart model is ideal if you like to make meals in advance and have dinner tonight and store leftovers for another day.

Types of Slow Cookers

Current models of **CROCK-POT®** slow cookers come equipped with many different features and benefits, from auto-cook programs, to stovetop-safe stoneware, to timed programming. Visit www.crockpot. com to find the slow cooker that best suits your needs and lifestyle.

Cooking, Stirring, and Food Safety

CROCK-POT® slow cookers are safe to leave unattended. The outer heating base may get hot as it cooks, but it should not pose a fire hazard. The heating element in the heating base functions at a low wattage and

is safe for your countertops.

Your slow cooker should be filled at least one-half to three-quarters full for most recipes unless otherwise instructed. Lean meats, such as chicken or pork tenderloin, will cook faster than meats with more connective tissue and fat, such as beef chuck or pork shoulder. Bone-in meats will take longer than boneless cuts. Typical slow cooker dishes take 7 to 8 hours to reach the simmer point on LOW and 3 to 4 hours on HIGH. Once the vegetables and meat begin to simmer and braise, their flavors will fully blend and the meat will become fall-off-the bone tender.

According to the United States Department of Agriculture, all bacteria are killed at a temperature of 165°F. It's important to follow the recommended cooking times and to avoid opening the lid often, especially early in the cooking process when heat is building up inside the unit. If you need to open the lid to check on your food or are adding additional ingredients, remember to allow additional cooking time, if necessary, to ensure food is thoroughly cooked and tender.

Large slow cookers, the 6- to 7-quart sizes, may benefit from a quick stir halfway through the cook time to help distribute heat and promote even cooking. It is usually unnecessary to stir at all since even ½ cup of liquid will help to distribute heat, and the crockery is the perfect medium for holding food at an even temperature throughout the cooking process.

Oven-Safe

All **CROCK-POT®** slow cooker removable crockery inserts may (without their lids) be used in

ovens at up to 400°F safely. Also, all **CROCK-POT®** crockery inserts are microwavable without their lids. If you own another brand slow cooker, please refer to your owner's manual for advice on oven and microwave safety.

Frozen Food

Frozen or partially frozen food can be cooked in a slow cooker; however, it will require a longer cooking time than the same recipe made with fresh food. Using an instant-read thermometer is recommended to ensure meat is completely cooked.

Pasta and Rice

If you're converting a recipe that calls for uncooked pasta, cook the

pasta according to the package directions just until tender before adding it to the slow cooker. If you are converting a recipe that calls for cooked rice, stir in the raw rice with other ingredients; add ¼ cup of extra liquid per ¼ cup of raw rice.

Beans

Beans must be softened completely before they're combined with sugar and/or acidic foods. Sugar and acid have a hardening effect on beans and will prevent softening. Fully cooked canned beans may be used as a substitute for dried beans.

Vegetables

Root vegetables often cook more slowly than meat. Cut vegetables into small pieces so that they cook at the same rate as the meat, large or small, lean or marbled. Place them near the sides or on the bottom of the stoneware so that they will cook more quickly.

Herbs

Fresh herbs add flavor and color when they're added at the end of the cooking time, but for dishes with shorter cook times, hearty

fresh herbs such as rosemary and thyme hold up well. If added at the beginning, the flavor of many fresh herbs lessen over long cook times. Ground and/or dried herbs and spices work well in slow cooking because they retain their flavor, and may be added at beginning.

The flavor power of all herbs and spices can vary greatly depending on their particular strength and shelf life. Use chili powders and garlic powder sparingly because they often intensify over long cook times. Always taste the finished dish and adjust the seasonings, including salt and pepper, before serving.

Liquids

It's not necessary to use more than ½ to 1 cup of liquid in most instances since the juices in meats and vegetables are retained in slow cooking more so than in conventional cooking. Excess liquid can be reduced and concentrated after slow cooking either on the stovetop or by removing meat and vegetables from stoneware, stirring in cornstarch or tapioca, and setting the slow cooker to HIGH. Cook on

HIGH for approximately 15 minutes or until the juices are thickened.

Milk

Milk, cream, and sour cream break down during extended cooking. When possible, add them during the last 15 to 30 minutes of cooking, until just heated through. Condensed soups may be substituted for milk and can cook for extended times.

Fish

Fish is delicate and it should be stirred in gently during the last 15 to 30 minutes of cooking time. Cook just until cooked through, and serve immediately.

SAVORY STARTERS

Moroccan Spiced Chicken Wings

¼ cup orange juice

3 tablespoons tomato paste

2 teaspoons ground cumin

1 teaspoon curry powder

1 teaspoon ground turmeric

½ teaspoon ground cinnamon

½ teaspoon ground ginger

1 teaspoon salt

1 tablespoon olive oil

5 pounds chicken wings, tips removed and split at joint

In **CROCK-POT®** slow cooker, combine juice, tomato paste, cumin, curry, turmeric, cinnamon, ginger and salt. Heat oil in large nonstick skillet over medium-high heat. Add wings and brown in several batches, about 6 minutes per batch. Transfer wings to **CROCK-POT®** slow cooker. Toss well to coat with sauce. Cover and cook on HIGH 3 to 3½ hours or until tender.

Makes 8 servings

Thai Coconut Chicken Meatballs

1 **pound ground chicken**

2 **green onions, chopped (both white and green parts)**

1 **clove garlic, minced**

2 **teaspoons toasted sesame oil**

1 **teaspoon fish sauce***

2 **teaspoons mirin (Japanese rice wine)***

1 **tablespoon canola oil**

½ **cup coconut milk**

¼ **cup chicken broth**

1 **teaspoon Thai red curry paste***

2 **teaspoons brown sugar**

2 **teaspoons lime juice**

1 **tablespoon cornstarch**

2 **tablespoons cold water**

Available in the Asian foods aisle of your local market.

1. In large bowl, combine chicken, green onions, garlic, sesame oil, fish sauce and mirin. Mix well with hands and form into 1½-inch meatballs.

2. Heat canola oil in skillet over medium heat. Add meatballs and cook, stirring until lightly browned. Alternatively, place meatballs on a cookie sheet and spray with cooking spray. Broil in oven until lightly browned.

3. Place meatballs in **CROCK-POT®** slow cooker. Add coconut milk, chicken broth, curry paste and sugar. Cover and cook on HIGH 3½ to 4 hours.

4. Add lime juice and mix well. In small bowl, whisk together cornstarch and cold water, stirring until it has consistency of heavy cream. Add to **CROCK-POT®** slow cooker. Cook, uncovered on HIGH 10 to 15 minutes longer or until sauce is thick enough to coat meatballs.

Makes 12 to 15 meatballs

Asian Lettuce Wraps

2 teaspoons canola oil

1½ pounds chicken breasts, chopped into ¼-inch pieces

2 leeks, chopped into ¼-inch pieces (both white and green parts)

1 cup shiitake mushrooms, stems removed and caps chopped into ¼-inch pieces

1 stalk celery, chopped into ¼-inch pieces

1 teaspoon toasted sesame oil*

1 tablespoon oyster sauce*

1 tablespoon soy sauce

¼ teaspoon black pepper

2 tablespoons water

1 bag (8 ounces) cole slaw or broccoli slaw mix

½ red bell pepper, seeded and cut into thin strips

½ pound shrimp, shelled, deveined and cut into ¼-inch pieces

3 tablespoons salted, dry roasted peanuts, lightly crushed

10 to 15 leaves crisp romaine lettuce

Hoisin sauce*

*Available in the Asian foods aisle of your local market.

1. Heat canola oil in small skillet over high heat. Add meat; cook and stir 4 to 5 minutes or until lightly browned on all sides. Transfer to **CROCK-POT®** slow cooker. Add leeks, mushrooms and celery. Stir in sesame oil, oyster sauce, soy sauce, pepper and water. Combine cole slaw and red pepper slices. Layer on top of meat mixture. Cover and cook on LOW 4 hours for chicken, 5 hours for pork.

2. With 20 minutes remaining in cooking time, stir in shrimp. When shrimp are cooked through, turn off heat and stir in crushed peanuts.

3. Wash lettuce leaves and pat dry. Remove white ribs. To serve wraps, spread hoisin sauce as desired on lettuce leaf. Spoon 1 to 2 tablespoons chicken mixture into leaf and roll up like a cigar.

Makes 10 to 15 wraps

Stuffed Baby Bell Peppers

- 1 tablespoon extra-virgin olive oil
- ½ medium onion, chopped
- ½ pound ground chicken
- ½ cup cooked white rice
- 1 tablespoon dry dill weed
- 3 tablespoons fresh parsley, chopped
- 1 tablespoon tomato paste, divided
- 2 tablespoons lemon juice
- ⅛ teaspoon black pepper
- ½ teaspoon salt
- 1 bag yellow and red baby bell peppers (16 to 18 peppers)
- ¼ cup vegetable, chicken or beef broth

1. Heat oil in medium skillet over medium heat. Add onion and cook, stirring, 2 minutes or until onion is translucent. Add ground meat and cook, stirring, 8 to 10 minutes or until thoroughly browned. Transfer meat to bowl. Mix in rice, dill, parsley, ½ tablespoon tomato paste, lemon juice, pepper and salt. Mix well.

2. Using paring knife, make slit in side of each pepper and run under cold water to remove any small seeds. Spoon 2 to 3 teaspoons meat mixture into each pepper.

3. In **CROCK-POT®** slow cooker, whisk together broth and remaining ½ tablespoon tomato paste. Arrange peppers in broth, slit side up. Cover and cook on LOW 5 hours.

Makes 16 to 18 servings

SAVORY STARTERS

Chicken and Asiago Stuffed Mushrooms

20 **large white mushrooms, stems removed and reserved**

3 **tablespoons extra-virgin olive oil, divided**

¼ **cup finely chopped onion**

2 **garlic cloves, minced**

¼ **cup Madeira wine**

½ **pound chicken sausage, removed from the casing or ½ pound ground chicken**

1 **cup grated Asiago cheese**

½ **cup Italian seasoned bread crumbs**

3 **tablespoons chopped fresh parsley**

½ **teaspoon salt**

¼ **teaspoon black pepper**

1. Lightly brush mushrooms with 1 tablespoon oil and set aside. Finely chop mushroom stems.

2. Heat remaining 2 tablespoons oil in large nonstick skillet over medium-high heat. Add onion and cook until just beginning to soften, about 1 minute. Add chopped mushroom stems and cook until beginning to brown, 5 to 6 minutes. Stir in garlic and cook 1 minute. Pour in Madeira and cook until evaporated, about 1 minute. Add sausage and cook, stirring, until no longer pink, 3 to 4 minutes. Remove from heat and cool 5 minutes. Stir in cheese, bread crumbs, parsley, salt and pepper.

3. Divide mushroom mixture among mushroom caps, pressing slightly on filling to compress. Place stuffed mushrooms in **CROCK-POT®** slow cooker; cover and cook on HIGH 2 hours or until mushrooms are tender and filling is cooked through.

Makes 4 to 5 servings

Asian Chicken "Fondue"

1 cup shiitake mushrooms, stems removed

2 cups chicken broth

1 tablespoon teriyaki sauce*

1 small leek, trimmed and chopped (both white and green parts)

1 head baby bok choy, trimmed and roughly chopped

1 tablespoon mirin (Japanese rice wine)*

2 tablespoons oyster sauce*

1 tablespoon canola oil

2 pounds boneless chicken breasts, cut into 1-inch cubes

Salt and black pepper

1 cup cubed butternut squash

1 can (8 ounces) baby corn, drained

1 can (8 ounces) water chestnuts, drained

1 tablespoon cornstarch

2 tablespoons cold water

Available in the Asian foods aisle of your local market.

1. In **CROCK-POT®** slow cooker, combine mushrooms, chicken broth, teriyaki sauce, leek, bok choy, mirin and oyster sauce.

2. Heat canola oil in skillet over medium heat. Season chicken with salt and pepper and add to skillet. Cook and stir until chicken is lightly browned on all sides. Transfer chicken to **CROCK-POT®** slow cooker. Add butternut squash. Cook on LOW 4½ to 5 hours.

3. With 20 minutes left in cooking time, add baby corn and water chestnuts. In small bowl, whisk together cornstarch and water to achieve consistency of heavy cream. Stir cornstarch mixture into **CROCK-POT®** slow cooker. Continue to cook, covered on LOW remaining 20 minutes.

4. Serve in **CROCK-POT®** slow cooker, set to WARM using bamboo skewers to spear meat and vegetables.

Makes 6 to 8 servings

18

Chicken Croustade

2 tablespoons canola oil

1½ pounds boneless, skinless chicken breasts, chopped into ¼-inch pieces

Salt and black pepper

1 shallot, minced

¼ cup white wine

1 large portobello mushroom cap, chopped into ¼-inch pieces

1 tablespoon fresh thyme

¼ teaspoon sweet paprika

¼ teaspoon cumin

¼ cup chicken broth

1 package (6 shells) puff pastry shells *or* ½ package (1 sheet) puff pastry dough*

1 egg yolk

2 tablespoons cream

3 tablespoons freshly grated Parmesan cheese

Minced chives, for garnish

If using puff pastry sheets, thaw, then slice each sheet into 9 squares; bake according to package directions.

1. Heat oil in large skillet over medium heat. Season chicken with salt and pepper and add to skillet. Brown chicken about 4 minutes; do not stir. Turn and brown other side. Place chicken in **CROCK-POT®** slow cooker.

2. Return skillet to low heat and add shallot. Cook 1 minute until shallot softens. Add white wine. Stir to scrape up any brown bits. Cook liquid down to 2 tablespoons, then add shallot mixture to **CROCK-POT®** slow cooker. Stir in mushroom, thyme, paprika, cumin, broth, salt and pepper; mix well. Cover and cook on LOW 3 hours.

3. With 1 hour left in cooking time, bake pastry shells according to package directions.

4. With 20 minutes left in cooking time, beat egg yolk and cream together. Add 1 tablespoon cooking liquid from chicken, beating constantly. Whisk mixture into **CROCK-POT®** slow cooker. Cook uncovered on LOW remaining 20 minutes. Stir in Parmesan. Serve chicken filling over puff pastry; garnish with chives.

Makes 6 to 9 servings

SAVORY STARTERS

Asian Barbecue Skewers

2 pounds boneless, skinless chicken thighs

½ cup soy sauce

⅓ cup packed brown sugar

2 tablespoons sesame oil

3 cloves garlic, minced

½ cup thinly sliced green onions

1 tablespoon toasted sesame seeds (optional)

1. Cut each thigh into 4 pieces about 1½ inches thick. Thread chicken onto 7-inch-long wooden skewers, folding thinner pieces, if necessary. Place skewers in **CROCK-POT®** slow cooker, layering as flat as possible.

2. Combine soy sauce, brown sugar, oil and garlic in small bowl. Reserve ⅓ cup sauce; set aside. Pour remaining sauce over skewers. Cover; cook on LOW 2 hours. Turn skewers over and cook 1 hour longer.

3. Transfer skewers to serving platter. Discard cooking liquid. Spoon on reserved sauce and sprinkle with sliced green onions and sesame seeds, if desired.

Makes 4 to 6 servings

Thai Chicken Wings

1 tablespoon peanut oil

5 pounds chicken wings, tips removed and split at the joint

½ cup coconut milk

1 tablespoon Thai green curry paste

1 tablespoon fish sauce

1 tablespoon sugar

¾ cup prepared spicy peanut sauce

1. Heat oil in large nonstick skillet over medium-high heat. Add chicken wings and brown in several batches, about 6 minutes per batch. Transfer wings to **CROCK-POT®** slow cooker as they are browned.

2. Stir in coconut milk, curry paste, fish sauce and sugar. Cover and cook on LOW 6 to 7 hours or on HIGH 3 to 3½ hours or until tender. Drain off cooking liquid and carefully stir in peanut sauce before serving.

Makes 8 servings

Asian Barbecue Skewers

SAVORY STARTERS

Chicken Liver Pâté

1½ **pounds chicken livers, trimmed of fat and membrane**

1 **small onion, thinly sliced**

3 **sprigs fresh thyme**

2 **cloves garlic, peeled and lightly smashed**

¼ **teaspoon salt**

3 **tablespoons cold butter, cut into 4 pieces**

2 **tablespoons heavy cream**

2 **tablespoons sherry**

½ **shallot, minced**

2 **tablespoons fresh parsley, minced**

1 **tablespoon sherry vinegar**

⅛ **teaspoon sugar**

Salt and black pepper

Melba toast crackers or toast points, for serving

1. Rinse chicken livers and pat dry. Place in **CROCK-POT®** slow cooker. Add onion, thyme, garlic and ¼ teaspoon salt. Add 1 tablespoon water, cover and cook on LOW 1½ hours.

2. Remove thyme sprigs and discard. Place chicken liver mixture in food processor and pulse to create coarse paste. Add butter pieces one at a time, pulsing to combine. Add cream and sherry and pulse until combined. Transfer mixture to bowl to serve immediately, or place in a small loaf pan and cover with plastic wrap, pressing wrap directly against surface of pâté. Refrigerate overnight until set.

3. Mix shallot, parsley, vinegar, sugar, salt and pepper and let sit for 2 to 3 minutes. Spread on top of pâté. Serve with Melba crackers or toast points.

Makes 8 to 10 servings

SAVORY STARTERS

Cranberry-Barbecue Chicken Wings

3 pounds chicken wings
  Salt and black pepper
1 jar (12 ounces) cranberry-orange relish
½ cup barbecue sauce
2 tablespoons quick-cooking tapioca
1 tablespoon prepared mustard

1. Preheat broiler. Cut off chicken wing tips; discard. Cut each wing in half at joint. Place chicken on rack in broiler pan; season with salt and pepper. Broil 4 to 5 inches from heat for 10 to 12 minutes or until browned, turning once. Transfer chicken to **CROCK-POT®** slow cooker.

2. Stir together relish, barbecue sauce, tapioca and mustard in small bowl. Pour over chicken. Cover; cook on LOW 4 to 5 hours.

Makes about 16 appetizer servings or 4 main dish servings

For a meal: *Serve one fourth of wings with rice for a main dish.*

Oriental Chicken Wings

32 pieces chicken wing drums and flats
1 cup chopped red onion
1 cup soy sauce
¾ cup packed light brown sugar
¼ cup dry cooking sherry
2 tablespoons chopped fresh ginger
2 cloves garlic, minced
  Chopped fresh chives (optional)

1. Preheat broiler. Broil chicken wing pieces about 5 minutes per side; transfer to **CROCK-POT®** slow cooker.

2. Combine onion, soy sauce, brown sugar, sherry, ginger and garlic in large bowl. Add to **CROCK-POT®** slow cooker; stir to blend well.

3. Cover and cook on LOW 5 to 6 hours or on HIGH 2 to 3 hours. Sprinkle with chives, if desired.

Makes 32 appetizers

Cranberry-Barbecue Chicken Wings

Angel Wings

1 can (10¾ ounces)
   condensed tomato soup,
   undiluted

¾ cup water

¼ cup packed brown sugar

2½ tablespoons balsamic
   vinegar

2 tablespoons chopped
   shallots

10 chicken wings

1. Combine soup, water, brown sugar, vinegar and shallots in **CROCK-POT®** slow cooker; mix well.

2. Add chicken wings; stir to coat with sauce. Cover; cook on LOW 5 to 6 hours or until cooked through.

Makes 2 servings

Honey-Glazed Chicken Wings

3 tablespoons vegetable oil,
   divided

3 pounds chicken wings,
   tips removed

1 cup honey

½ cup soy sauce

1 clove garlic, minced

2 tablespoons tomato paste

2 teaspoons water

1 teaspoon sugar

1 teaspoon black pepper

1. Heat 1½ tablespoons oil in skillet over medium heat until hot. Brown chicken wings on each side in batches to prevent crowding. Turn each piece as it browns, about 1 to 2 minutes per side. Transfer with slotted spoon to **CROCK-POT®** slow cooker.

2. Combine honey, soy sauce, remaining 1½ tablespoons vegetable oil, and garlic in medium bowl. Whisk in tomato paste, water, sugar and pepper. Pour sauce over chicken. Cover; cook on LOW 6 to 8 hours or on HIGH 3 to 4 hours.

Makes 6 to 8 servings

Angel Wings

Asian-Spiced Chicken Wings

3 pounds chicken wings

1 cup packed brown sugar

1 cup soy sauce

½ cup ketchup

2 teaspoons fresh ginger, minced

2 cloves garlic, minced

¼ cup dry sherry

½ cup hoisin sauce

1 tablespoon fresh lime juice

3 tablespoons sesame seeds, toasted

¼ cup green onions, thinly sliced

1. Broil the chicken wings 10 minutes on each side or until browned. Transfer chicken wings to **CROCK-POT®** slow cooker. Add remaining ingredients, except hoisin sauce, lime juice, sesame seeds and green onions; stir thoroughly. Cover; cook on LOW 5 to 6 hours or on HIGH 2 to 3 hours or until wings are no longer pink, stirring once halfway through the cooking time to baste the wings with sauce.

2. Remove wings from stoneware. Remove ¼ cup of cooking liquid (discard the rest). Combine liquid with hoisin sauce and lime juice. Drizzle mixture over wings.

3. Before serving, sprinkle wings with sesame seeds and green onions.

Note: *Chicken wings are always crowd pleasers. Garnishing them with toasted sesame seeds and green onions gives these appetizers added crunch and contrasting color.*

Tip: *For 5-, 6- or 7-quart **CROCK-POT®** slow cooker, increase chicken wings to 5 pounds.*

Makes 10 to 16 wings

IMPRESS YOUR GUESTS

Bistro Chicken in Rich Cream Sauce

4 skinless, bone-in chicken breast halves, rinsed and patted dry (about 3 pounds total)

½ cup dry white wine, divided

1 tablespoon or ½ packet (0.7 ounces) Italian salad dressing and seasoning mix

½ teaspoon dried oregano

1 can (10¾ ounces) condensed cream of chicken soup, undiluted

3 ounces cream cheese, cut into cubes

¼ teaspoon salt

⅛ teaspoon black pepper

2 tablespoons chopped fresh parsley

1. Coat **CROCK-POT®** slow cooker with nonstick cooking spray. Arrange chicken in single layer in bottom, overlapping slightly. Pour ¼ cup wine over chicken. Sprinkle evenly with salad dressing mix and oregano. Cover; cook on LOW 5 to 6 hours or on HIGH 3 hours.

2. Transfer chicken to plate with slotted spoon. Turn **CROCK-POT®** slow cooker to HIGH. Whisk soup, cream cheese, salt and pepper into cooking liquid. (Mixture will be a bit lumpy.) Arrange chicken on top. Cover; cook 15 to 20 minutes longer to heat through.

3. Transfer chicken to shallow pasta bowl. Add remaining ¼ cup wine to sauce and whisk until smooth. To serve, spoon sauce around chicken, and garnish with parsley.

Makes 4 servings

32

Chicken and Artichoke-Parmesan Dressing

2 cans (14 ounces each) quartered artichoke hearts, drained and coarsely chopped

4 ounces herb-seasoned stuffing

1½ cups frozen seasoning-blend vegetables, thawed*

¾ cup mayonnaise

¾ cup grated Parmesan cheese, divided

1 large egg, beaten

½ teaspoon paprika

½ teaspoon dried oregano

½ teaspoon salt

¼ teaspoon black pepper

6 bone-in chicken breast halves, rinsed and patted dry (about 3½ pounds)

Grated Parmesan cheese (optional)

Seasoning-blend vegetables are a mixture of chopped bell peppers, onions and celery. If you're unable to find frozen vegetables, use ½ cup of each fresh vegetable.

1. Coat **CROCK-POT®** slow cooker with cooking spray. Combine artichokes, stuffing, vegetables, mayonnaise, all but 1 tablespoon Parmesan and egg in large bowl. Stir gently to blend well. Transfer mixture to **CROCK-POT®** slow cooker.

2. Combine paprika, oregano, salt and pepper in small bowl. Rub evenly onto chicken. Arrange chicken on top of artichoke mixture in **CROCK-POT®** slow cooker, overlapping pieces slightly. Cover; cook on HIGH 3 hours.

3. Transfer chicken to serving platter. Cover with foil to keep warm. Stir artichoke mixture in **CROCK-POT®** slow cooker. Sprinkle evenly with remaining 1 tablespoon Parmesan. Cook, uncovered, 20 to 25 minutes, or until thickened. Serve dressing with chicken.

Makes 6 servings

Coq au Vin

2 cups frozen pearl onions, thawed

4 slices thick-cut bacon, crisp-cooked and crumbled

1 cup sliced button mushrooms

1 clove garlic, minced

1 teaspoon dried thyme

⅛ teaspoon black pepper

6 boneless, skinless chicken breasts (about 2 pounds)

½ cup dry red wine

¾ cup reduced-sodium chicken broth

¼ cup tomato paste

3 tablespoons all-purpose flour

Hot cooked egg noodles (optional)

1. Layer onions, bacon, mushrooms, garlic, thyme, pepper, chicken, wine and broth in **CROCK-POT®** slow cooker.

2. Cover; cook on LOW 6 to 8 hours.

3. Remove chicken and vegetables; cover and keep warm. Ladle ½ cup cooking liquid into small bowl; cool slightly. Mix reserved liquid, tomato paste and flour until smooth; stir into **CROCK-POT®** slow cooker. Cook; uncovered, on HIGH 15 minutes or until thickened. Serve over hot noodles, if desired.

Makes 6 servings

Cook's Nook: *Coq au Vin is a classic French dish that is made with bone-in chicken, salt pork or bacon, brandy, red wine and herbs. The dish originated when farmers needed a way to cook old chickens that could no longer breed. A slow, moist cooking method was needed to tenderize the tough old birds.*

Stuffed Chicken Breasts

6 **boneless, skinless chicken breasts**

8 **ounces feta cheese, crumbled**

3 **cups chopped fresh spinach leaves**

⅓ **cup oil-packed sun-dried tomatoes, drained and chopped**

1 **teaspoon minced lemon peel**

1 **teaspoon dried basil, oregano or mint**

½ **teaspoon garlic powder**

Freshly ground black pepper, to taste

1 **can (15 ounces) diced tomatoes, undrained**

½ **cup oil-cured olives***

Hot cooked polenta

*If using pitted olives, add to CROCK-POT® slow cooker in the final hour of cooking.

1. Place 1 chicken breast between 2 pieces of plastic wrap. Using tenderizer mallet or back of skillet, pound breast until about ¼-inch thick. Repeat with remaining chicken.

2. Combine feta, spinach, sun-dried tomatoes, lemon peel, basil, garlic powder and pepper in medium bowl.

3. Lay pounded chicken, smooth side down, on work surface. Place about 2 tablespoons feta mixture on wide end of breast. Roll tightly. Repeat with remaining chicken.

4. Place rolled chicken, seam side down, in **CROCK-POT®** slow cooker. Top with diced tomatoes with juice and olives. Cover; cook on LOW 5½ to 6 hours or on HIGH 4 hours. Serve with polenta.

Makes 6 servings

Chicken Tangier

2 tablespoons dried oregano

2 teaspoons seasoning salt

2 teaspoons puréed garlic

¼ teaspoon black pepper

3 pounds skinless chicken thighs

8 thin slices lemon

½ cup dry white wine

2 tablespoons olive oil

1 cup pitted prunes

¼ cup currants or raisins

½ cup pitted green olives

2 tablespoons capers

Hot cooked noodles or rice

Chopped fresh parsley or cilantro, to garnish

1. Stir together oregano, salt, garlic and pepper in small bowl. Rub mixture onto chicken, coating on all sides.

2. Spray inside of **CROCK-POT®** slow cooker with cooking spray and add chicken. Tuck lemon slices between chicken pieces. Pour wine over chicken and sprinkle olive oil on top. Add prunes, currants, olives and capers. Cover and cook on LOW 7 to 8 hours or on HIGH 4 to 5 hours.

3. To serve, spoon over cooked noodles or rice and sprinkle with chopped fresh parsley or cilantro.

Makes 8 servings

Indian-Style Apricot Chicken

6 chicken thighs,
  rinsed and patted dry

¼ teaspoon salt

¼ teaspoon black pepper

1 tablespoon vegetable oil

1 large onion, chopped

2 cloves garlic, minced

2 tablespoons grated fresh
  ginger

½ teaspoon ground
  cinnamon

⅛ teaspoon ground allspice

1 can (14½ ounces) diced
  tomatoes, undrained

1 cup chicken broth

1 package (8 ounces) dried
  apricots

1 pinch saffron threads
  (optional)

Hot basmati rice

2 tablespoons chopped
  fresh parsley

1. Coat **CROCK-POT®** slow cooker with nonstick cooking spray. Season chicken with salt and pepper. Heat oil in large skillet over medium-high heat until hot. Brown chicken on all sides. Transfer to **CROCK-POT®** slow cooker.

2. Add onion to skillet. Cook and stir 3 to 5 minutes or until translucent. Stir in garlic, ginger, cinnamon and allspice. Cook and stir 15 to 30 seconds longer or until mixture is fragrant. Add tomatoes with juice and broth. Cook 2 to 3 minutes or until mixture is heated through. Pour into **CROCK-POT®** slow cooker.

3. Add apricots and saffron, if desired. Cover; cook on LOW 5 to 6 hours or on HIGH 3 to 3½ hours or until chicken is tender. Add salt and pepper, if desired. Serve with basmati rice and garnish with chopped parsley.

Makes 4 to 6 servings

Note: *Use skinless chicken thighs, if desired. To skin chicken easily, grasp skin with paper towel and pull away. Repeat with fresh paper towel for each piece of chicken, discarding skins and towels.*

Greek Chicken and Orzo

2 medium green bell peppers, cut into thin strips

1 cup chopped onion

2 teaspoons extra-virgin olive oil

8 skinless chicken thighs, rinsed and patted dry

1 tablespoon dried oregano

½ teaspoon dried rosemary

½ teaspoon garlic powder

¾ teaspoon salt, divided

⅜ teaspoon black pepper, divided

8 ounces uncooked dry orzo pasta

Juice and grated peel of 1 medium lemon

½ cup water

2 ounces crumbled feta cheese (optional)

Chopped fresh parsley (optional)

1. Coat **CROCK-POT®** slow cooker with nonstick cooking spray. Add bell peppers and onion.

2. Heat oil in large skillet over medium-high heat until hot. Brown chicken on both sides. Transfer to **CROCK-POT®** slow cooker, overlapping slightly if necessary. Sprinkle chicken with oregano, rosemary, garlic powder, ¼ teaspoon salt and ⅛ teaspoon black pepper. Cover; cook on LOW 5 to 6 hours or on HIGH 3 hours.

3. Transfer chicken to separate plate. Turn **CROCK-POT®** slow cooker to high. Stir orzo, lemon juice, lemon peel, water and remaining ½ teaspoon salt and ¼ teaspoon black pepper into **CROCK-POT®** slow cooker. Top with chicken. Cover; cook on HIGH 30 minutes or until pasta is done. Garnish with feta cheese and parsley, if desired.

Makes 4 servings

Note: *To skin chicken easily, grasp skin with paper towel and pull away. Repeat with fresh paper towel for each piece of chicken, discarding skins and towels.*

Forty-Clove Chicken

1 cut-up whole chicken
(about 3 pounds)

Salt and black pepper

1 to 2 tablespoons olive oil

¼ cup dry white wine

2 tablespoons chopped
fresh parsley or
2 teaspoons dried parsley
flakes

2 tablespoons dry vermouth

2 teaspoons dried basil

1 teaspoon dried oregano

Pinch red pepper flakes

40 cloves garlic (about
2 heads), peeled*

4 stalks celery, sliced

Juice and peel of 1 lemon

Fresh herbs

*The whole garlic bulb is called a
head.

1. Remove skin from chicken. Sprinkle chicken with salt and pepper. Heat oil in large skillet over medium heat. Add chicken; brown on all sides. Remove to platter.

2. Combine wine, parsley, vermouth, basil, oregano and red pepper flakes in large bowl. Add garlic and celery; coat well. Transfer garlic and celery to **CROCK-POT®** slow cooker with slotted spoon. Add chicken to remaining herb mixture; coat well. Place chicken on top of celery mixture in **CROCK-POT®** slow cooker. Sprinkle lemon juice and peel over chicken. Cover; cook on LOW 6 hours.

3. Sprinkle with fresh herbs before serving.

Makes 4 to 6 servings

Basque Chicken with Peppers

1 whole chicken (about 4 pounds), cut into 8 pieces

Salt and black pepper

1½ tablespoons olive oil

1 onion, chopped

1 medium green bell pepper, sliced

1 medium yellow bell pepper, sliced

1 medium red bell pepper, sliced

1 package (8 ounces) button or cremini mushrooms, halved

2 large cloves garlic, minced

½ cup Rioja wine

1 can (14½ ounces) stewed tomatoes, drained

3 tablespoons tomato paste

½ cup chicken stock

1 sprig marjoram

1 teaspoon smoked paprika

4 ounces diced prosciutto

1. Rinse chicken and pat dry. Season with salt and pepper. Heat olive oil in large skillet over medium-high heat. Add chicken pieces in batches and brown well on all sides. Transfer chicken to **CROCK-POT®** slow cooker.

2. When all chicken has been browned, reduce heat under skillet and add onion. Cook and stir 3 minutes or until softened. Add bell peppers and mushrooms; cook and stir 3 minutes. Stir in garlic, wine, tomatoes, tomato paste, chicken stock, marjoram and paprika. Season to taste with salt and pepper. Bring to simmer; simmer 3 to 4 minutes. Pour mixture over chicken in **CROCK-POT®** slow cooker. Cover and cook on HIGH 4 hours or until chicken is tender.

3. Remove chicken to deep platter or serving bowl with tongs. Spoon vegetables and sauce over chicken. Sprinkle with prosciutto and serve.

Makes 4 to 6 servings

Chicken Parmesan with Eggplant

6 **boneless, skinless chicken breasts**

2 **eggs**

2 **teaspoons salt**

2 **teaspoons black pepper**

2 **cups Italian bread crumbs**

½ **cup olive oil**

½ **cup (1 stick) butter**

2 **small eggplants, cut into ¾-inch thick slices**

1½ **cups grated Parmesan cheese, divided**

2½ **cups tomato-basil sauce, divided**

1 **pound sliced or shredded mozzarella cheese**

1. Slice chicken breasts in half lengthwise. Cut each half lengthwise again to get 4 (¾-inch) slices.

2. Combine eggs, salt and pepper in medium bowl. Place bread crumbs in separate bowl or on plate. Dip each chicken piece in egg, then coat in bread crumbs.

3. Heat oil and butter in skillet over medium heat until hot. Brown breaded chicken on all sides, turning as pieces brown. Transfer to paper-towel-lined plate to drain excess oil.

4. Layer eggplant on bottom of **CROCK-POT®** slow cooker. Add ¾ cup Parmesan cheese and 1¼ cups sauce. Arrange chicken on sauce. Add remaining Parmesan cheese and sauce. Top with mozzarella cheese. Cover; cook on LOW 6 hours or on HIGH 2 to 4 hours.

Makes 6 to 8 servings

Easy Cheesy Aruban-Inspired Chicken

1 can (14½ ounces) diced tomatoes in sauce

½ cup chicken broth

¼ cup ketchup

2 teaspoons yellow mustard

1 teaspoon Worcestershire sauce

¾ teaspoon hot sauce

3 cloves garlic, crushed

½ teaspoon salt

¼ teaspoon pepper

1 large onion, thinly sliced

1 large green bell pepper, seeded, cored and thinly sliced

¼ cup sliced black olives

¼ cup raisins

1 tablespoon capers

4 to 6 chicken thighs or 4 boneless, skinless breasts

1½ cups (6 ounces) shredded Edam or Gouda cheese

2 tablespoons chopped flat-leaf parsley

Hot cooked rice (optional)

1. Coat **CROCK-POT®** slow cooker with nonstick cooking spray. Add tomatoes in sauce, broth, ketchup, mustard, Worcestershire sauce, hot sauce, garlic, salt and pepper. Stir well to combine.

2. Add onion, bell pepper, olives, raisins and capers. Stir well to combine.

3. Add chicken. Spoon sauce mixture over chicken until well coated. Cover; cook on HIGH 3 to 4 hours or until chicken is no longer pink.

4. Turn off **CROCK-POT®** slow cooker and uncover. Sprinkle cheese and parsley over chicken. Cover and let stand 3 to 5 minutes or until cheese is melted. Serve over rice, if desired.

Makes 4 servings

Curry Chicken with Peaches and Raisins

2 peaches, peeled and sliced into ¼-inch slices, reserving 8 slices for garnish

Lemon juice

4 skinless chicken thighs (or 2 boneless, skinless chicken breasts)

Salt and black pepper, to taste

1 tablespoon olive oil

⅓ cup raisins, chopped, or ⅓ cup currants, whole

1 shallot, thinly sliced

1 tablespoon grated fresh ginger

2 garlic cloves, crushed

½ teaspoon curry powder

1 teaspoon ground cumin

½ teaspoon whole cloves

¼ cup chicken stock

1 tablespoon cider vinegar

¼ teaspoon ground red pepper (optional)

1 teaspoon cornstarch (optional)

Fresh cilantro leaves (optional)

Hot cooked rice (optional)

1. Toss 8 slices of peaches with lemon juice to coat and refrigerate. Rinse, dry and season chicken with salt and black pepper.

2. Heat olive oil in skillet until hot. Add chicken and lightly brown, about 3 minutes per side. Transfer to **CROCK-POT®** slow cooker. Top with remaining peaches, raisins and shallots.

3. Whisk together ginger, garlic, curry, cumin, cloves, stock, vinegar and ground red pepper, if desired. Pour mixture over chicken. Cover; cook on LOW 5 hours or on HIGH 3 to 3½ hours.

4. Transfer chicken to serving dish. Stir cornstarch into sauce to thicken, if desired. Spoon peaches, raisins and sauce over chicken. Top with reserved peaches and cilantro, if desired. Serve over rice, if desired.

Makes 2 servings

Citrus Mangoretto Chicken

4 **boneless skinless chicken breasts (about 1 pound)**

1 **large ripe mango, peeled and diced**

3 **tablespoons freshly squeezed lime juice**

1 **tablespoon grated lime peel**

¼ **cup Amaretto liqueur**

1 **tablespoon chopped fresh rosemary or 1 teaspoon crushed dried rosemary**

1 **cup chicken broth**

1 **tablespoon water**

2 **teaspoons cornstarch**

1. Place 2 chicken breasts side by side on bottom of **CROCK-POT®** slow cooker.

2. Combine mango, lime juice, lime peel, Amaretto and rosemary in medium bowl. Spread half of mango mixture over chicken in **CROCK-POT®** slow cooker. Lay remaining 2 chicken breasts on top crosswise, and spread with remaining mango mixture. Carefully pour broth around edges of chicken. Cover; cook on LOW 3 to 4 hours.

3. Combine water and cornstarch. Stir into cooking liquid. Cook 15 minutes longer or until sauce has thickened. Serve mango and sauce over chicken.

Makes 4 servings

Variation: *Chill chicken and sauce. Serve over salad greens.*

Basil Chicken Merlot with Wild Mushrooms

3 tablespoons extra-virgin olive oil, divided

1 roasting chicken (about 3 pounds), skinned and cut into individual pieces

1½ cups thickly sliced cremini mushrooms

1 medium yellow onion, diced

2 cloves garlic, minced

1 cup chicken broth

1 can (6 ounces) tomato paste

⅓ cup Merlot or other dry red wine

2 teaspoons sugar

1 teaspoon ground oregano

¼ teaspoon salt

¼ teaspoon black pepper

2 tablespoons minced fresh basil

3 cups cooked ziti pasta, drained

Grated Romano cheese (optional)

1. Heat 1½ to 2 tablespoons oil in skillet over medium heat until hot. Brown one-half of chicken pieces on each side about 3 to 5 minutes, turning once. Remove with slotted spoon and repeat with remaining chicken. Set chicken aside.

2. Heat remaining oil in skillet and add mushrooms, onion and garlic. Cook and stir 7 to 8 minutes or until onions are soft. Transfer to **CROCK-POT®** slow cooker. Top with reserved chicken.

3. Combine broth, tomato paste, wine, sugar, oregano, salt and pepper in medium bowl. Pour sauce over chicken. Cover; cook on LOW 7 to 9 hours or on HIGH 3 to 4 hours.

4. Stir in fresh basil. Place pasta in large serving bowl or on platter. Ladle chicken and mushrooms over pasta and spoon extra sauce over all. Garnish with Romano cheese, if desired.

Makes 4 to 6 servings

55

Jamaica-Me-Crazy Chicken Tropicale

2 medium sweet potatoes, peeled and cut into 2-inch pieces

1 can (8 ounces) water chestnuts, drained and sliced

1 cup golden raisins

1 can (20 ounces) pineapple tidbits in pineapple juice, drained and juice reserved

4 boneless skinless chicken breasts

4 teaspoons Jamaican jerk seasoning, or to taste

¼ cup dried onion flakes

3 tablespoons grated fresh ginger

2 tablespoons Worcestershire sauce

1 tablespoon grated lime peel

1 teaspoon cumin seed, slightly crushed

Hot cooked rice (optional)

1. Place sweet potatoes in **CROCK-POT®** slow cooker. Add water chestnuts, raisins and pineapple tidbits; mix well.

2. Sprinkle chicken with jerk seasoning. Place chicken over potato mixture.

3. Combine reserved pineapple juice, onion flakes, ginger, Worcestershire, lime peel and cumin in small bowl. Pour mixture over chicken. Cover; cook on LOW 7 to 9 hours or on HIGH 3 to 4 hours, or until chicken and potatoes are fork-tender. Serve with rice, if desired.

Makes 4 servings

Sesame Chicken

4 chicken legs, bone in (or 4 thighs and 4 drumsticks)

4 chicken breasts, bone in

1 cup rice flour

8 teaspoons sesame seeds

Salt and black pepper

Vegetable oil

1 cup chicken broth

½ cup chopped celery

¼ cup chopped onion

1 teaspoon dried tarragon

¼ cup cornstarch

¼ cup water

1½ cups sour cream

1. Cut through joints to separate thighs and drumsticks. Split breasts in half. Mix rice flour, sesame seeds, salt and pepper in medium bowl. Dip chicken pieces in mixture to coat.

2. Heat oil in skillet over medium heat until hot. Brown chicken on all sides, turning as it browns. Transfer to paper towel-lined plate with slotted spoon to drain excess fat. Place in **CROCK-POT®** slow cooker.

3. Add broth, celery, onion and tarragon. Cover; cook on LOW 7 to 8 hours or on HIGH 3 to 4 hours.

4. Turn **CROCK-POT®** slow cooker to HIGH. Combine cornstarch and water in small bowl. Add sour cream. Mix well to combine. Add to **CROCK-POT®** slow cooker. Stir gently to combine. Cover; cook on HIGH 15 to 20 minutes, or until thickened.

Makes 4 to 6 servings

Autumn Herbed Chicken with Fennel and Squash

3 to 4 pounds chicken thighs

Salt and black pepper, to taste

All-purpose flour, as needed

2 tablespoons olive oil

1 fennel bulb, thinly sliced

½ butternut squash, peeled, seeded and cut into ¾-inch cubes

1 teaspoon dried thyme

¾ cup walnuts (optional)

¾ cup chicken broth

½ cup apple cider or juice

Cooked rice or pasta

¼ cup fresh basil, sliced into ribbons

2 teaspoons fresh rosemary, finely minced

1. Season chicken on all sides with salt and pepper, then lightly coat with flour. Heat oil in skillet over medium heat until hot. Brown chicken in batches to prevent crowding. Brown on each side 3 to 5 minutes, turning once. Remove with slotted spoon. Transfer to **CROCK-POT®** slow cooker.

2. Add fennel, squash and thyme. Stir well to combine. Add walnuts, if desired, broth and cider. Cover; cook on LOW 5 to 7 hours or on HIGH 2½ to 4½ hours.

3. Serve over rice or pasta and garnish with basil and fresh rosemary.

Makes 6 servings

EVERYDAY GOURMET

Autumn Chicken

1 can (14 ounces) whole
artichoke hearts, drained

1 can (14 ounces) whole
mushrooms, divided

12 boneless, skinless chicken
breasts

1 jar (6½ ounces) marinated
artichoke hearts, with
liquid

¾ cup white wine

½ cup balsamic vinaigrette

Hot cooked noodles

Paprika, for garnish
(optional)

Spread whole artichokes over bottom of **CROCK-POT®** slow cooker. Top with half the mushrooms. Layer chicken over mushrooms. Add marinated artichoke hearts with liquid. Add remaining mushrooms. Pour in wine and vinaigrette. Cover; cook on LOW 4 to 5 hours. Serve over noodles. Garnish with paprika, if desired.

Makes 10 to 12 servings

Cerveza Chicken Enchilada Casserole

2 cups water

1 stalk celery, chopped

1 small carrot, peeled and chopped

1 bottle (12 ounces) Mexican beer, divided

Juice of 1 lime

1 teaspoon salt

1½ pounds boneless, skinless chicken breasts

1 can (19 ounces) enchilada sauce, divided

7 ounces white corn tortilla chips

½ medium onion, chopped

3 cups shredded Cheddar cheese

Sour cream, sliced olives and cilantro (optional)

1. Heat water, celery, carrot, 1 cup beer, lime juice and salt in saucepan over high heat until boiling. Add chicken breasts; reduce heat to simmer. Cook until chicken is cooked through, about 12 to 14 minutes. Remove; cool and shred into bite-sized pieces.

2. Spoon ½ cup enchilada sauce in bottom of **CROCK-POT®** slow cooker. Place tortilla chips in 1 layer over sauce. Cover with ⅓ shredded chicken. Sprinkle ⅓ chopped onion over chicken. Add 1 cup cheese, spreading evenly. Pour ½ cup enchilada sauce over cheese. Repeat layering process 2 more times, pouring remaining beer over casserole before adding last layer of cheese.

3. Cook on LOW 3½ to 4 hours. Garnish with sour cream, sliced olives and cilantro, if desired.

Makes 4 to 6 servings

Cashew Chicken

6 boneless, skinless chicken breasts

1½ cups cashews

1 cup sliced mushrooms

1 cup sliced celery

1 can (10¾ ounces) condensed cream of mushroom soup, undiluted

¼ cup chopped green onion

2 tablespoons butter

1½ tablespoons soy sauce

Hot cooked rice

1. Combine chicken, cashews, mushrooms, celery, soup, green onion, butter and soy sauce in **CROCK-POT®** slow cooker.

2. Cover; cook on LOW 6 to 8 hours or on HIGH 4 to 6 hours or until done. Serve over rice.

Note: *Time spent in the kitchen cooking with your kids is time well spent. You can share the value of preparing wholesome, comforting, nurturing foods while equipping them with the skills to create their own food traditions in the future. Even young children can participate in family meal preparation. Just remember these basics: Always make sure children are well-supervised in the kitchen. Only adults should use sharp utensils, plug in or turn on electric appliances or handle hot foods. Be sure to only assign tasks that the child can do and feel good about.*

Makes 6 servings

Dijon Chicken Thighs with Artichoke Sauce

⅓ cup Dijon mustard

2 tablespoons chopped garlic

½ teaspoon dried tarragon

2½ pounds chicken thighs (about 8), skinned

1 cup chopped onion

1 cup sliced mushrooms

1 jar (12 ounces) quartered marinated artichoke hearts, undrained

¼ cup chopped fresh parsley

1. Combine mustard, garlic and tarragon in large bowl. Add chicken thighs and toss to coat. Transfer to **CROCK-POT®** slow cooker.

2. Add onion, mushrooms and artichokes with liquid. Cover; cook on LOW 6 to 8 hours or on HIGH 4 hours or until chicken is tender. Stir in parsley just before serving.

Makes 8 servings

Serving suggestion: *Serve with hot fettuccine that has been tossed with butter and parsley.*

Note: *To skin chicken easily, grasp skin with paper towel and pull away. Repeat with fresh paper towel for each piece of chicken, discarding skins and towels.*

Mediterranean Chicken Breasts and Wild Rice

1 **pound boneless, skinless chicken breasts, lightly pounded**

Kosher salt, to taste

Black pepper, to taste

1 **cup white and wild rice blend**

10 **cloves garlic, smashed**

½ **cup oil-packed or dry sun-dried tomatoes***

½ **cup capers, drained**

2 **cups water**

½ **cup fresh-squeezed lemon juice**

¼ **cup extra-virgin olive oil**

*If using dry sun-dried tomatoes, soak in boiling water to soften before chopping.

1. Season chicken with salt and black pepper. Place in **CROCK-POT®** slow cooker. Add rice, garlic, tomatoes and capers; stir well.

2. Mix water, lemon juice and oil in small mixing bowl. Pour mixture over rice and chicken. Stir once to coat chicken. Cover; cook on LOW 8 hours.

Makes 4 servings

Chicken Teriyaki

1 **pound boneless, skinless chicken tenders**

1 **can (6 ounces) pineapple juice**

¼ **cup soy sauce**

1 **tablespoon sugar**

1 **tablespoon minced fresh ginger**

1 **tablespoon minced garlic**

1 **tablespoon vegetable oil**

1 **tablespoon molasses**

24 **cherry tomatoes (optional)**

2 **cups hot cooked rice**

Combine all ingredients except rice in **CROCK-POT®** slow cooker. Cover; cook on LOW 2 hours or until chicken is tender. Serve chicken and sauce over rice.

Makes 4 servings

Chicken in Honey Sauce

4 **to 6 boneless, skinless chicken breasts**

Salt

Black pepper

2 **cups honey**

1 **cup soy sauce**

½ **cup ketchup**

¼ **cup oil**

2 **cloves garlic, minced**

Sesame seeds

1. Place chicken in **CROCK-POT®** slow cooker; season with salt and pepper.

2. Combine honey, soy sauce, ketchup, oil and garlic in medium bowl. Pour over chicken. Cover; cook on LOW 6 to 8 hours or on HIGH 3 to 4 hours.

3. Garnish with sesame seeds before serving.

Makes 4 to 6 servings

Chicken Teriyaki

Thai Chicken

2½ **pounds chicken pieces**

1 **cup hot salsa**

¼ **cup peanut butter**

2 **tablespoons lime juice**

1 **tablespoon soy sauce**

1 **teaspoon minced fresh ginger**

Cooked white rice, for serving

½ **cup peanuts, chopped**

2 **tablespoons chopped fresh cilantro**

1. Place chicken in **CROCK-POT®** slow cooker. In a bowl, mix together salsa, peanut butter, lime juice, soy sauce and ginger. Pour over chicken.

2. Cover; cook on LOW 8 to 9 hours or on HIGH 3 to 4 hours or until done.

3. To serve, place chicken over rice, pour sauce over chicken; sprinkle with peanuts and cilantro.

Makes 6 servings

Provençal Lemon and Olive Chicken

2 cups chopped onion

8 skinless chicken thighs (about 2½ pounds)

1 lemon, thinly sliced and seeds removed

1 cup pitted green olives

1 tablespoon olive brine from jar *or* 1 tablespoon white vinegar

2 teaspoons herbes de Provence

1 bay leaf

½ teaspoon salt

⅛ teaspoon black pepper

1 cup chicken broth

½ cup minced fresh parsley

1. Place onion in **CROCK-POT®** slow cooker. Arrange chicken thighs over onion. Place lemon slice on each thigh. Add olives, brine, herbes de Provence, bay leaf, salt and pepper. Slowly pour in chicken broth.

2. Cover; cook on LOW 5 to 6 hours or on HIGH 3 to 3½ hours or until chicken is tender. Stir in parsley before serving.

Makes 8 servings

Note: *To skin chicken easily, grasp skin with paper towel and pull away. Repeat with fresh paper towel for each piece of chicken, discarding skins and towels.*

Chicken & Rice

3 cans (10¾ ounces each)
  condensed cream of
  chicken soup, undiluted

2 cups uncooked instant
  rice

1 cup water

1 pound boneless, skinless
  chicken breasts *or*
  chicken breast tenders

½ teaspoon salt

¼ teaspoon paprika

¼ teaspoon black pepper

½ cup diced celery

Combine soup, rice and water in **CROCK-POT®** slow cooker. Add chicken; sprinkle with salt, paprika and pepper. Sprinkle celery over chicken. Cover; cook on LOW 6 to 8 hours or on HIGH 3 to 4 hours.

Makes 4 servings

Herbed Artichoke Chicken

1½ **pounds boneless, skinless chicken breasts**

1 **can (14 ounces) tomatoes, drained and diced**

1 **can (14 ounces) artichoke hearts in water, drained**

1 **small onion, chopped**

½ **cup kalamata olives, pitted and sliced**

1 **cup fat-free chicken broth**

¼ **cup dry white wine**

3 **tablespoons quick-cooking tapioca**

2 **teaspoons curry powder**

1 **tablespoon chopped fresh Italian parsley**

1 **teaspoon dried sweet basil**

1 **teaspoon dried thyme leaves**

½ **teaspoon salt**

½ **teaspoon freshly ground black pepper**

1. Combine chicken, tomatoes, artichokes, onion, olives, broth, wine, tapioca, curry powder, parsley, basil, thyme, salt and pepper in **CROCK-POT®** slow cooker. Mix thoroughly.

2. Cover; cook on LOW for 6 to 8 hours or on HIGH for 3½ to 4 hours or until chicken is no longer pink in center.

Makes 6 servings

Tip: *For a larger crowd, use a 5-, 6- or 7-quart* **CROCK-POT®** *slow cooker and double all ingredients, except the chicken broth and white wine. Increase the chicken broth and white wine by one half.*

Chicken Pilaf

2 pounds chopped cooked chicken

2 cans (8 ounces each) tomato sauce

2½ cups water

1⅓ cups uncooked long-grain converted rice

1 cup chopped onion

1 cup chopped celery

1 cup chopped green bell pepper

⅔ cup sliced black olives

¼ cup sliced almonds

¼ cup (½ stick) margarine *or* butter

2 cloves garlic, minced

2½ teaspoons salt

½ teaspoon ground allspice

½ teaspoon ground turmeric

¼ teaspoon curry powder

¼ teaspoon black pepper

1. Combine all ingredients in **CROCK-POT®** slow cooker; stir well.

2. Cover; cook on LOW 6 to 8 hours or on HIGH 3 to 4 hours.

Makes 10 servings

Chicken Parisienne

6 boneless, skinless chicken breasts (about 1½ pounds), cubed

½ teaspoon salt

½ teaspoon black pepper

½ teaspoon paprika

1 can (10¾ ounces) condensed cream of mushroom *or* cream of chicken soup, undiluted

2 cans (4 ounces each) sliced mushrooms, drained

½ cup dry white wine

1 cup sour cream

6 cups hot cooked egg noodles

1. Place chicken in **CROCK-POT®** slow cooker. Sprinkle with salt, pepper and paprika. Add soup, mushrooms and wine to slow cooker; mix well.

2. Cover; cook on HIGH 2 to 3 hours.

3. Stir in sour cream during last 30 minutes of cooking. Serve over noodles. Garnish as desired.

Makes 6 servings

Serving suggestion: *Try this dish over rice instead of noodles.*

Chipotle Chicken Casserole

1 **pound boneless, skinless chicken thighs, cut into cubes**

1 **teaspoon salt**

1 **teaspoon ground cumin**

1 **bay leaf**

1 **chipotle pepper in adobo sauce, minced**

1 **medium onion, diced**

1 **can (15 ounces) navy beans, drained and rinsed**

1 **can (15 ounces) black beans, drained and rinsed**

1 **can (14½ ounces) crushed tomatoes, undrained**

1½ **cups chicken broth**

½ **cup orange juice**

¼ **cup chopped fresh cilantro, for garnish (optional)**

Combine chicken, salt, cumin, bay leaf, chipotle pepper, onion, beans, tomatoes with juice, broth and orange juice in **CROCK-POT®** slow cooker. Cover; cook on LOW 7 to 8 hours or on HIGH 3½ to 4 hours. Remove bay leaf before serving. Garnish with cilantro, if desired.

Makes 6 servings

WEEKNIGHT WINNERS

Roast Chicken with Peas, Prosciutto and Cream

1 **cut-up whole chicken (about 2½ pounds)**

   Salt and black pepper, to taste

5 **ounces prosciutto, diced**

1 **small white onion, finely chopped**

½ **cup dry white wine**

1 **package (10 ounces) frozen peas**

½ **cup heavy cream**

1½ **tablespoons cornstarch**

2 **tablespoons water**

4 **cups farfalle pasta, cooked al dente**

1. Season chicken pieces with salt and pepper. Combine chicken, prosciutto, onion and wine in **CROCK-POT®** slow cooker. Cover; cook on HIGH 3½ to 4 hours or on LOW 8 to 10 hours, until chicken is no longer pink in center.

2. During last 30 minutes of cooking, add frozen peas and heavy cream to cooking liquid.

3. Remove chicken with slotted spoon. Carve meat and set aside on warmed platter.

4. Combine cornstarch and water. Add to cooking liquid in **CROCK-POT®** slow cooker. Cover; cook on HIGH 10 to 15 minutes or until thickened.

5. To serve, spoon pasta onto individual plates. Place chicken on pasta and top each portion with sauce.

Makes 6 servings

Curry Chicken with Mango and Red Pepper

6 boneless, skinless chicken thighs or breasts

Salt and black pepper, to taste

Olive oil

1 bag (8 ounces) frozen mango chunks, thawed and drained

2 red bell peppers, cored, seeded and diced

⅓ cup raisins

1 shallot, thinly sliced

¾ cup chicken broth

1 tablespoon cider vinegar

2 cloves garlic, crushed

4 thin slices fresh ginger

1 teaspoon ground cumin

½ teaspoon curry powder

½ teaspoon whole cloves

¼ teaspoon ground red pepper (optional)

Fresh cilantro (optional)

1. Rinse, dry and season chicken with salt and pepper.

2. Heat oil in skillet over medium heat until hot. Add chicken and lightly brown, about 3 minutes per side. Transfer to **CROCK-POT®** slow cooker.

3. Add mango, bell peppers, raisins, and shallot. Combine remaining ingredients in small bowl, and pour over chicken. Cover; cook on LOW 6 to 8 hours or on HIGH 3 to 4 hours.

4. To serve, spoon mangos, raisins and cooking liquid onto chicken. Garnish with cilantro, if desired.

Makes 4 servings

Chicken and Mushroom Fettuccine Alfredo

1½ pounds chicken breast cutlets, rinsed, patted dry and cut into strips

2 packages (8 ounces each) cremini mushrooms, cut into thirds

½ teaspoon salt

½ teaspoon black pepper

¼ teaspoon garlic powder

2 packages (8 ounces each) cream cheese, cut into pieces

2 sticks butter, cut into pieces

1½ cups grated Parmesan cheese, plus additional for serving

1½ cups whole milk

1 box (8 ounces) fettucine noodles

1. Spray **CROCK-POT®** slow cooker with nonstick cooking spray. Add chicken strips in single layer. Distribute mushrooms evenly over chicken. Sprinkle salt, pepper, and garlic powder over mushrooms.

2. In medium saucepan over medium heat, stir together cream cheese, butter, cheese and milk. Whisk continuously until smooth and heated through. Pour mixture over mushrooms, pushing down any mushrooms that float to top. Cover and cook on LOW 4 to 5 hours.

3. Cook fettuccine according to package directions. Drain. Add fettuccine to **CROCK-POT®** slow cooker and toss gently with sauce. Serve with Parmesan cheese.

Makes 6 to 8 servings

Spanish Paella with Chicken and Sausage

1 **tablespoon olive oil**

2 **pounds chicken thighs**

1 **medium onion, chopped**

1 **clove garlic, minced**

1 **pound hot smoked sausages, sliced**

1 **can (14½ ounces) stewed tomatoes**

1 **cup Arborio rice**

4 **cups chicken broth**

1 **pinch saffron (optional)**

½ **cup frozen peas, thawed**

1. Heat oil in large skillet over medium-high heat. Brown chicken on all sides and place in **CROCK-POT®** slow cooker.

2. Add onions to skillet, cook and stir until translucent. Stir in garlic, sausages, tomatoes, rice, chicken broth and saffron. Pour mixture over chicken.

3. Cover and cook on HIGH 3 to 4 hours or until chicken and rice are tender. Remove chicken pieces to platter and fluff rice with fork. Stir in peas. Spoon rice onto platter with chicken.

Makes 4 servings

Chicken Cacciatore

¼ cup vegetable oil

2½ to 3 pounds chicken tenders, cut into bite-size pieces

1 can (28 ounces) crushed Italian-style tomatoes

2 cans (8 ounces each) Italian-style tomato sauce

1 medium onion, chopped

1 can (4 ounces) sliced mushrooms, drained

2 cloves garlic, minced

1 teaspoon salt

1 teaspoon dried oregano leaves

½ teaspoon dried thyme leaves

½ teaspoon black pepper

Hot cooked spaghetti or rice

1. Heat oil in large skillet over medium-low heat. Brown chicken on all sides. Drain excess fat.

2. Transfer chicken to **CROCK-POT®** slow cooker. Add remaining ingredients except spaghetti. Cover; cook on LOW 6 to 8 hours. Serve over spaghetti.

Makes 6 to 8 servings

Braised Italian Chicken with Tomatoes and Olives

2 pounds boneless, skinless chicken thighs

1 teaspoon kosher salt

½ teaspoon black pepper

½ cup all-purpose flour

Olive oil

1 can (14½ ounces) diced tomatoes, drained

⅓ cup dry red wine

⅓ cup pitted quartered Kalamata olives

1 clove garlic, minced

1 teaspoon chopped fresh rosemary

½ teaspoon crushed red pepper flakes

Cooked linguini or spaghetti

Grated or shredded Parmesan cheese (optional)

1. Season chicken with salt and pepper. Spread flour on plate, and lightly dredge chicken in flour, coating both sides.

2. Heat oil in skillet over medium heat until hot. Sear chicken in 2 or 3 batches until well browned on both sides. Use additional oil as needed to prevent sticking. Transfer to **CROCK-POT®** slow cooker.

3. Add tomatoes, wine, olives and garlic. Cover; cook on LOW 4 to 5 hours.

4. Add rosemary and red pepper flakes; stir in. Cover; cook on LOW 1 hour longer. Serve over linguini. Garnish with cheese, if desired.

Makes 4 servings

Traditional Cassoulet

1 small onion, finely chopped

2 cloves garlic, finely chopped

½ cup finely chopped, peeled carrots

½ cup roughly chopped, seeded tomatoes

1 can (about 15 ounces) cannellini beans, drained and rinsed

¼ cup bread crumbs

2 tablespoons finely chopped, fresh majoram leaves

2 tablespoons finely chopped, fresh parsley leaves

2 tablespoons olive oil

1½ pounds chicken thighs

½ pound bulk pork sausage

½ cup dry white wine

½ cup chicken broth

1. Combine onion, garlic, carrots, tomatoes, beans, bread crumbs and fresh herbs in **CROCK-POT®** slow cooker.

2. Heat olive oil in large skillet over medium-high heat. Add chicken in single layer (in batches, if necessary) and cook 3 to 4 minutes per side or until brown. Place chicken on top of mixture in **CROCK-POT®** slow cooker. Add sausage to skillet. Cook, stirring to break up meat, until cooked through. Transfer sausage to **CROCK-POT®** slow cooker with slotted spoon.

3. Return skillet to medium-high heat. Add wine and chicken broth to skillet and stir to scrape up any browned bits. Bring to a boil and cook until liquid is reduced to about one third its original volume. Remove from heat.

4. Pour reduced liquid over contents of **CROCK-POT®** slow cooker. Cover and cook on LOW 6 to 7 hours or on HIGH 3½ hours.

Makes 4 servings

Greek Chicken Pitas with Creamy Mustard Sauce

Filling

1 medium green bell pepper, cored, seeded and sliced into ½-inch strips

1 medium onion, cut into 8 wedges

1 pound boneless skinless chicken breasts, rinsed and patted dry

1 tablespoon extra-virgin olive oil

2 teaspoons dried Greek seasoning blend

¼ teaspoon salt

Sauce

¼ cup plain fat-free yogurt

¼ cup mayonnaise

1 tablespoon prepared mustard

¼ teaspoon salt

4 whole pita rounds

½ cup crumbled feta cheese

Optional toppings: Sliced cucumbers, sliced tomatoes, Kalamata olives

1. Coat **CROCK-POT®** slow cooker with nonstick cooking spray. Place bell pepper and onion in bottom. Add chicken, and drizzle on oil. Sprinkle evenly with seasoning and ¼ teaspoon salt. Cover; cook on HIGH 1¾ hours or until chicken is no longer pink and vegetables are crisp-tender.

2. Remove chicken and slice. Remove vegetables using slotted spoon.

3. To prepare sauce: Combine yogurt, mayonnaise, mustard and ¼ teaspoon salt in small bowl. Whisk until smooth.

4. Warm pitas according to package directions. Cut in half, and fill with chicken, sauce, vegetables and feta cheese. Top as desired.

Makes 4 servings

Chicken and Spicy Black Bean Tacos

1 can (15 ounces) black beans, drained and rinsed

1 can (10 ounces) tomatoes with mild green chiles, drained

1½ teaspoons chili powder

¾ teaspoon ground cumin

1 tablespoon plus 1 teaspoon extra-virgin olive oil, divided

12 ounces boneless, skinless chicken breasts, rinsed and patted dry

12 crisp corn taco shells

Optional toppings: shredded lettuce, diced tomatoes, shredded cheese, sour cream, ripe olives

1. Coat **CROCK-POT®** slow cooker with nonstick cooking spray. Add beans and tomatoes with chiles. Blend chili powder and cumin with 1 teaspoon oil and rub onto chicken breasts. Place chicken in **CROCK-POT®** slow cooker. Cover; cook on HIGH 1¾ hours.

2. Remove chicken and slice. Transfer bean mixture to bowl using slotted spoon. Stir in 1 tablespoon oil.

3. To serve, warm taco shells according to package directions. Fill with equal amounts of bean mixture and chicken. Add toppings as desired.

Makes 4 servings

Thai-Style Chicken Thighs

1 teaspoon ground ginger

½ teaspoon salt

¼ teaspoon ground red pepper

6 bone-in chicken thighs (about 2¼ pounds), skin removed

1 medium onion, chopped

3 cloves garlic, minced

⅓ cup canned coconut milk

¼ cup peanut butter

2 tablespoons soy sauce

1 tablespoon cornstarch

2 tablespoons water

3 cups hot cooked couscous *or* yellow rice

¼ cup chopped cilantro

Lime wedges (optional)

1. Combine ginger, salt and red pepper; sprinkle over meaty sides of chicken. Place onion and garlic in **CROCK-POT®** slow cooker; top with chicken. Whisk together coconut milk, peanut butter and soy sauce; pour over chicken. Cover; cook on LOW 6 to 7 hours or on HIGH 3 to 4 hours or until chicken is tender.

2. With slotted spoon, transfer chicken to serving bowl; cover with foil to keep warm. Turn **CROCK-POT®** slow cooker to high. Combine cornstarch and water until smooth. Stir into **CROCK-POT®** slow cooker; cover and cook 15 minutes or until sauce is slightly thickened. Spoon sauce over chicken. Serve chicken over couscous; top with cilantro. Garnish with lime wedges.

Makes 6 servings

Cajun Chicken and Shrimp Creole

1 **pound skinless chicken thighs**

1 **red bell pepper, chopped**

1 **large onion, chopped**

1 **rib celery, diced**

1 **can (15 ounces) stewed tomatoes, undrained and chopped**

1 **clove garlic, minced**

1 **tablespoon sugar**

1 **teaspoon paprika**

1 **teaspoon Cajun seasoning**

1 **teaspoon salt**

1 **teaspoon freshly ground black pepper**

1 **pound shelled shrimp, deveined and cleaned**

1 **tablespoon fresh lemon juice**

Louisiana-style hot sauce to taste

1 **cup prepared quick-cooking rice**

1. Place chicken thighs in **CROCK-POT®** slow cooker. Add bell pepper, onion, celery, tomatoes with juice, garlic, sugar, paprika, Cajun seasoning, salt and pepper.

2. Cover; cook on LOW 8 to 10 hours or on HIGH 4 to 5 hours.

3. In the last hour of cooking, add shrimp, lemon juice and hot sauce. Serve over hot rice.

Makes 6 servings

Note: *Enjoy the full flavors of chicken, shrimp and spices in this delicious creole!*

Tip: *For a 5-, 6- or 7-quart* **CROCK-POT®** *slow cooker, double all ingredients.*

Chicken Curry

2 boneless skinless chicken breasts, cut into ¾-inch pieces

1 cup coarsely chopped apple, divided

1 small onion, sliced

3 tablespoons raisins

1 clove garlic, minced

1 teaspoon curry powder

¼ teaspoon ground ginger

⅓ cup water

1½ teaspoons chicken bouillon granules

1½ teaspoons all-purpose flour

¼ cup sour cream

½ teaspoon cornstarch

½ cup uncooked white rice

1. Combine chicken, ¾ cup apple, onion, raisins, garlic, curry powder and ginger in **CROCK-POT®** slow cooker. Combine water and bouillon granules in small bowl until dissolved. Stir in flour until smooth. Add to **CROCK-POT®** slow cooker. Cover; cook on LOW 3½ to 4 hours or until onion is tender and chicken is cooked through.

2. Combine sour cream and cornstarch in large bowl. Turn off **CROCK-POT®** slow cooker. Transfer all cooking liquid from chicken mixture to sour cream mixture; stir until combined. Stir mixture back into **CROCK-POT®** slow cooker. Cover; let stand 5 to 10 minutes or until sauce is heated through.

3. Meanwhile, cook rice according to package directions. Serve chicken curry over rice; garnish with remaining ¼ cup apple.

Makes 2 servings

Hint: *Sprinkle with green onion slivers just before serving.*

Creamy Chicken and Mushrooms

1 teaspoon salt

½ teaspoon black pepper

¼ teaspoon paprika

3 boneless, skinless chicken breasts, cut into 1-inch pieces

1½ cups sliced fresh mushrooms

½ cup sliced green onions

1¾ teaspoons chicken bouillon granules

1 cup dry white wine

½ cup water

1 can (5 ounces) evaporated milk

5 teaspoons cornstarch

Hot cooked rice

1. Combine salt, pepper and paprika in small bowl; sprinkle over chicken.

2. Layer chicken, mushrooms, green onions and bouillon granules in **CROCK-POT®** slow cooker. Pour wine and water over top. Cover; cook on LOW 5 to 6 hours or on HIGH 3 hours. Remove chicken and vegetables; cover to keep warm.

3. Combine evaporated milk and cornstarch in small saucepan, stirring until smooth. Add 2 cups liquid from **CROCK-POT®** slow cooker; bring to a boil. Boil 1 minute or until thickened, stirring constantly. Serve chicken over rice and top with sauce.

Makes 3 to 4 servings

Chinese Cashew Chicken

1 can (16 ounces) bean sprouts, drained

2 cups sliced cooked chicken

1 can (10¾ ounces) condensed cream of mushroom soup, undiluted

1 cup sliced celery

½ cup chopped green onions with tops

1 can (4 ounces) sliced mushrooms, drained

3 tablespoons butter

1 tablespoon soy sauce

1 cup whole cashews

Hot cooked rice

1. Combine bean sprouts, chicken, soup, celery, onions, mushrooms, butter and soy sauce in **CROCK-POT®** slow cooker; mix well. Cover; cook on LOW 4 to 6 hours or on HIGH 2 to 3 hours.

2. Stir in cashews just before serving. Serve over rice.

Makes 4 servings

Tip: *For easier preparation, cut up the ingredients for this* **CROCK-POT®** *slow cooker recipe the night before. Don't place the* **CROCK-POT®** *stoneware in the refrigerator. Instead, wrap the chicken and vegetables separately, and store in the refrigerator.*

Tender Asian-Style Chicken

6 to 8 boneless, skinless chicken thighs

¼ cup all-purpose flour

½ teaspoon black pepper

1 tablespoon vegetable oil

¼ cup soy sauce

2 tablespoons rice wine vinegar

2 tablespoons ketchup

1 tablespoon brown sugar

1 clove garlic, minced

½ teaspoon grated fresh ginger *or* ¼ teaspoon ground ginger

¼ teaspoon red pepper flakes

Hot cooked rice

Chopped fresh cilantro (optional)

1. Trim fat from chicken. Combine flour and black pepper in resealable food storage bag. Add chicken; shake to coat with flour mixture.

2. Heat oil in large skillet over medium-high heat. Brown chicken about 2 minutes on each side. Place chicken in **CROCK-POT®** slow cooker. Combine soy sauce, vinegar, ketchup, sugar, garlic, ginger and pepper flakes in small bowl; pour over chicken. Cook on LOW 5 to 6 hours. Serve with rice and garnish with cilantro, if desired.

Makes 4 to 6 servings

Chicken and Ham with Biscuits

2 cans (10¾ ounces each) condensed cream of mushroom soup, undiluted

2 cups diced ham

2 cups diced boneless chicken

1 package (12 ounces) frozen peas and onions

1 package (8 ounces) frozen corn

½ cup chopped celery

¼ teaspoon dried marjoram

¼ teaspoon dried thyme

2 tablespoons cornstarch

2 teaspoons water

1 to 2 cans refrigerated buttermilk biscuits

4 tablespoons (½ stick) butter, melted

1. Combine soup, ham, chicken, frozen vegetables, celery, marjoram and thyme in **CROCK-POT®** slow cooker. Cover; cook on LOW 4 to 5 hours or on HIGH 1 to 3 hours.

2. Mix cornstarch and water together in bowl. Stir into **CROCK-POT®** slow cooker. Cook 10 to 15 minutes longer or until mixture has thickened.

3. Meanwhile, place biscuits on baking sheet and brush with butter. Bake according to package directions until biscuits are golden brown.

4. To serve, ladle stew into bowls and top with warm biscuit.

Makes 8 to 10 servings

SOUPS, STEWS & CHILIES

Chipotle Chicken Stew

1 **pound boneless, skinless chicken thighs, cut into cubes**
1 **can (15 ounces) navy beans, drained and rinsed**
1 **can (15 ounces) black beans, drained and rinsed**
1 **can (14½ ounces) crushed tomatoes, undrained**
1½ **cups chicken broth**
½ **cup orange juice**
1 **medium onion, diced**
1 **chipotle pepper in adobo sauce, minced**
1 **teaspoon salt**
1 **teaspoon ground cumin**
1 **bay leaf**
  Cilantro sprigs (optional)

1. Combine chicken, beans, tomatoes with juice, broth, orange juice, onion, chipotle pepper, salt, cumin and bay leaf in **CROCK-POT®** slow cooker.

2. Cover; cook on LOW 7 to 8 hours or on HIGH 3½ to 4 hours. Remove bay leaf before serving. Garnish with cilantro sprigs, if desired.

Makes 6 servings

Chicken and Chile Pepper Stew

1 **pound boneless, skinless chicken thighs, cut into ½-inch pieces**

1 **pound small potatoes, cut lengthwise into halves, then crosswise into slices**

1 **cup chopped onion**

2 **poblano chile peppers, seeded and cut into ½-inch pieces***

1 **jalapeño pepper, seeded and finely chopped***

3 **cloves garlic, minced**

3 **cups fat-free reduced-sodium chicken broth**

1 **can (about 14 ounces) no-salt-added diced tomatoes**

2 **tablespoons chili powder**

1 **teaspoon dried oregano**

*Chile peppers can sting and irritate the skin, so wear rubber gloves when handling peppers and do not touch your eyes.

1. Place chicken, potatoes, onion, poblano peppers, jalapeño pepper and garlic in **CROCK-POT®** slow cooker.

2. Stir together broth, tomatoes, chili powder and oregano in large bowl. Pour broth mixture over chicken mixture in **CROCK-POT®** slow cooker; mix well. Cover; cook on LOW 8 to 9 hours.

Makes 6 servings

Black and White Chili

1 pound chicken tenders, cut into ¾-inch pieces

1 cup coarsely chopped onion

1 can (about 15 ounces) Great Northern beans, drained

1 can (about 15 ounces) black beans, drained

1 can (about 14 ounces) Mexican-style stewed tomatoes, undrained

2 tablespoons Texas-style chili powder seasoning mix

1. Spray large skillet with cooking spray; heat over medium heat until hot. Add chicken and onion; cook and stir 5 minutes or until chicken is browned.

2. Combine chicken mixture, beans, tomatoes with juice and chili seasoning in **CROCK-POT®** slow cooker. Cover; cook on LOW 4 to 4½ hours.

Makes 6 servings

Serving Suggestion: *For a change of pace, this delicious chili is excellent served over cooked rice or pasta.*

Chicken Tortilla Soup

1 pound boneless, skinless chicken breasts

2 cans (15 ounces each) diced tomatoes, undrained

1 can (4 ounces) chopped mild green chiles, drained

½ to 1 cup chicken broth, divided

1 yellow onion, diced

2 cloves garlic, minced

1 teaspoon ground cumin

Salt and black pepper, to taste

4 corn tortillas, sliced into ¼-inch strips

2 tablespoons chopped fresh cilantro

½ cup shredded Monterey Jack cheese

1 avocado, peeled, diced and tossed with lime juice to prevent browning

Lime wedges

1. Place chicken in **CROCK-POT®** slow cooker. Combine tomatoes with juice, chiles, ½ cup broth, onion, garlic and cumin in small bowl. Pour mixture over chicken. Cover; cook on LOW 6 hours or on HIGH 3 hours, or until chicken is tender.

2. Remove chicken from **CROCK-POT®** slow cooker. Shred with 2 forks. Return to cooking liquid. Adjust seasonings, adding salt, pepper and more broth, as desired.

3. Just before serving, add tortillas and cilantro to **CROCK-POT®** slow cooker. Stir to blend. Serve in soup bowls, topping each serving with cheese, avocado and a squeeze of lime juice.

Makes 4 servings

Chicken and Sweet Potato Stew

4 boneless, skinless chicken breasts, cut into bite-size pieces

2 medium sweet potatoes, peeled and cubed

2 medium Yukon Gold potatoes, peeled and cubed

2 medium carrots, peeled and cut into ½-inch slices

1 can (28 ounces) whole stewed tomatoes

1 teaspoon salt

1 teaspoon paprika

1 teaspoon celery seeds

½ teaspoon black pepper

⅛ teaspoon ground cinnamon

⅛ teaspoon ground nutmeg

1 cup nonfat, low-sodium chicken broth

¼ cup fresh basil, chopped

1. Combine chicken, potatoes, carrots, tomatoes, salt, paprika, celery seeds, pepper, cinnamon, nutmeg and broth in **CROCK-POT®** slow cooker.

2. Cover; cook on LOW for 6 to 8 hours or on HIGH for 3 to 4 hours.

3. Sprinkle with basil just before serving.

Makes 6 servings

Note: *This light stew has an Indian influence and offers excellent flavor without the fat.*

Chicken and Vegetable Chowder

1 **pound boneless, skinless chicken breasts, cut into 1-inch pieces**

1 **can (about 14 ounces) reduced-sodium chicken broth**

1 **can (10¾ ounces) condensed cream of potato soup, undiluted**

1 **package (10 ounces) frozen broccoli florets, thawed**

1 **cup sliced carrots**

1 **jar (4½ ounces) sliced mushrooms, drained**

½ **cup chopped onion**

½ **cup whole kernel corn**

2 **cloves garlic, minced**

½ **teaspoon dried thyme leaves**

⅓ **cup half-and-half**

1. Combine chicken, broth, soup, broccoli, carrots, mushrooms, onion, corn, garlic and thyme in **CROCK-POT®** slow cooker; mix well. Cover; cook on LOW 5 to 6 hours.

2. Stir in half-and-half. Cover; cook on HIGH 15 minutes or until heated through.

Makes 6 servings

Variation: *Add ½ cup (2 ounces) shredded Swiss or Cheddar cheese just before serving, stirring over LOW heat until melted.*

Chicken Stew with Herb Dumplings

2 cans (about 14 ounces each) chicken broth, divided

2 cups sliced carrots

1 cup chopped onion

1 large green bell pepper, sliced

½ cup sliced celery

⅔ cup all-purpose flour

1 pound boneless, skinless chicken breasts, cut into 1-inch pieces

1 large potato, unpeeled and cut into 1-inch pieces

6 ounces mushrooms, halved

¾ cup frozen peas

1 teaspoon dried basil

¾ teaspoon dried rosemary

¼ teaspoon dried tarragon

¾ to 1 teaspoon salt

¼ teaspoon black pepper

¼ cup whipping cream

Herb Dumplings

1 cup biscuit baking mix

¼ teaspoon dried basil

¼ teaspoon dried rosemary

⅛ teaspoon dried tarragon

⅓ cup milk

1. Reserve 1 cup chicken broth. Combine carrots, onion, bell pepper, celery and remaining chicken broth in **CROCK-POT®** slow cooker. Cover; cook on LOW 2 hours.

2. Stir remaining 1 cup broth into flour until smooth. Stir into **CROCK-POT®** slow cooker. Add chicken, potato, mushrooms, peas, 1 teaspoon basil, ¾ teaspoon rosemary and ¼ teaspoon tarragon to **CROCK-POT®** slow cooker. Cover; cook 4 hours or until vegetables are tender and chicken is tender. Stir in salt, black pepper and cream.

3. Combine baking mix, ¼ teaspoon basil, ¼ teaspoon rosemary and ⅛ teaspoon tarragon in small bowl. Stir in milk to form soft dough. Spoon dumpling mixture on top of stew in 4 large spoonfuls. Cook, uncovered, 30 minutes. Cover; cook 30 to 45 minutes or until dumplings are firm and toothpick inserted in center comes out clean. Serve in shallow bowls.

Makes 4 servings

Chicken and Black Bean Chili

1 pound boneless, skinless chicken thighs, cut into 1-inch chunks

2 teaspoons chili powder

2 teaspoons ground cumin

¾ teaspoon salt

1 green bell pepper, diced

1 small onion, chopped

3 cloves garlic, minced

1 can (about 14 ounces) diced tomatoes, undrained

1 cup chunky salsa

1 can (about 15 ounces) black beans, drained and rinsed

Optional toppings: sour cream, diced ripe avocado, shredded Cheddar cheese, sliced green onions or chopped cilantro and/or crushed tortilla or corn chips (optional)

1. Combine chicken, chili powder, cumin and salt in **CROCK-POT®** slow cooker; toss to coat.

2. Add bell pepper, onion and garlic; mix well. Stir in tomatoes and salsa. Cover; cook on LOW 5 to 6 hours or on HIGH 2½ to 3 hours or until chicken is tender.

3. Increase heat to HIGH; stir in beans. Cover; cook 5 to 10 minutes or until beans are heated through. Ladle into bowls; serve with desired toppings.

Makes 4 servings

Smoky Chipotle Cassoulet

1 **pound boneless, skinless chicken thighs, cubed**

1 **teaspoon salt**

1 **teaspoon ground cumin**

1 **bay leaf**

1 **chipotle pepper in adobo sauce, minced**

1 **medium onion, diced**

1 **can (15 ounces) navy beans, rinsed and drained**

1 **can (15 ounces) black beans, rinsed and drained**

1 **can (14½ ounces) crushed tomatoes, undrained**

1½ **cups chicken stock**

½ **cup fresh-squeezed orange juice**

¼ **cup chopped fresh cilantro (optional)**

1. Combine all ingredients, except cilantro, in **CROCK-POT®** slow cooker. Cover; cook on LOW 7 to 8 hours or on HIGH 4 to 5 hours.

2. Remove bay leaf before serving. Garnish with cilantro, if desired.

Makes 6 servings

Quatro Frijoles con Pollo Cantaro

1 cup pitted black olives, drained

1 pound boneless, skinless chicken breasts, cubed*

1 can (16 ounces) garbanzo beans, drained and rinsed

1 can (16 ounces) Great Northern or navy beans, drained and rinsed

1 can (15 ounces) cannellini beans, drained and rinsed

1 can (16 ounces) red kidney beans, drained and rinsed

1 can (7 ounces) chopped mild green chiles, drained

2 cups chicken stock, plus extra as needed

2 tablespoons canola or olive oil

1 cup minced onions

2 teaspoons minced garlic

1½ teaspoons ground cumin

Hot sauce, to taste

Salt and black pepper, to taste

2 cups crushed corn chips

6 ounces Monterey Jack cheese, grated

Turkey, pork or beef can be substituted for chicken.

1. Combine olives, chicken, beans, chiles and chicken stock in **CROCK-POT®** slow cooker. Mix well; set aside.

2. Heat oil in large skillet over medium-high heat. Cook onion, garlic and cumin until onions are soft, stirring frequently. Add to chicken mixture. Cover; cook on LOW 4 to 5 hours. Check liquid about halfway through, adding more hot broth as needed.

3. Taste and add hot sauce, salt and pepper. Serve in warm bowls and garnish with corn chips and cheese.

Makes 6 servings

White Bean Chili

Nonstick cooking spray

1 **pound ground chicken**

3 **cups coarsely chopped celery**

1 **can (28 ounces) whole tomatoes, undrained and coarsely chopped**

1 **can (15½ ounces) Great Northern beans, rinsed and drained**

1½ **cups coarsely chopped onions**

1 **cup chicken broth**

3 **cloves garlic, minced**

4 **teaspoons chili powder**

1½ **teaspoons ground cumin**

¾ **teaspoon ground allspice**

¾ **teaspoon ground cinnamon**

½ **teaspoon black pepper**

1. Spray large nonstick skillet with nonstick cooking spray; brown chicken over medium-high heat, stirring to break up chicken.

2. Combine chicken, celery, tomatoes with juice, beans, onions, broth, garlic, chili powder, cumin, allspice, cinnamon and pepper in **CROCK-POT®** slow cooker. Cover; cook on LOW 5½ to 6 hours.

Makes 6 servings

Greek-Style Chicken Stew

2 cups sliced mushrooms

2 cups cubed peeled eggplant

1¼ cups reduced-sodium chicken broth

¾ cup coarsely chopped onion

2 cloves garlic, minced

1½ teaspoons all-purpose flour

1 teaspoon dried oregano

½ teaspoon dried basil

½ teaspoon dried thyme

6 skinless chicken breasts, about 2 pounds

Additional all-purpose flour

3 tablespoons dry sherry or reduced-sodium chicken broth

¼ teaspoon salt

¼ teaspoon black pepper

1 can (14 ounces) artichoke hearts, drained

12 ounces uncooked wide egg noodles

1. Combine mushrooms, eggplant, broth, onion, garlic, flour, oregano, basil and thyme in **CROCK-POT®** slow cooker. Cover; cook on HIGH 1 hour.

2. Coat chicken very lightly with flour. Generously spray large nonstick skillet with cooking spray; heat over medium heat until hot. Cook chicken 10 to 15 minutes or until browned on all sides.

3. Remove vegetables to bowl with slotted spoon. Layer chicken in **CROCK-POT®** slow cooker; return vegetables to **CROCK-POT®** slow cooker. Add sherry, salt and pepper. Reduce heat to LOW. Cover; cook 6 to 6½ hours or until chicken is no longer pink in center and vegetables are tender.

4. Stir in artichokes; cover and cook 45 minutes to 1 hour or until heated through. Cook noodles according to package directions. Serve chicken stew over noodles.

Makes 6 servings

133

Chinese Chicken Stew

1 **pound boneless, skinless chicken thighs, cut into 1-inch pieces**

1 **teaspoon Chinese five-spice powder***

½ **to ¾ teaspoon red pepper flakes**

1 **tablespoon peanut or vegetable oil**

1 **large onion, coarsely chopped**

1 **package (8 ounces) fresh mushrooms, sliced**

2 **cloves garlic, minced**

1 **can (about 14 ounces) chicken broth, divided**

1 **tablespoon cornstarch**

1 **large red bell pepper, cut into ¾-inch pieces**

2 **tablespoons soy sauce**

2 **large green onions, cut into ½-inch pieces**

1 **tablespoon sesame oil**

3 **cups hot cooked white rice (optional)**

¼ **cup coarsely chopped fresh cilantro (optional)**

*Chinese five-spice powder is a blend of cinnamon, cloves, fennel seed, anise and Szechuan peppercorns. It is available in most supermarkets and at Asian grocery stores.

1. Toss chicken with five-spice powder and red pepper flakes in small bowl. Heat peanut oil in large skillet. Add onion and chicken; cook and stir about 5 minutes or until chicken is browned. Add mushrooms and garlic; cook and stir until chicken is no longer pink.

2. Combine ¼ cup broth and cornstarch in small bowl; set aside. Place cooked chicken mixture, remaining broth, bell pepper and soy sauce in **CROCK-POT®** slow cooker. Cover; cook on LOW 3½ hours or until peppers are tender.

3. Stir in cornstarch mixture, green onions and sesame oil. Cook 30 to 45 minutes or until thickened. Ladle into soup bowls; scoop ½ cup rice into each bowl and sprinkle with cilantro, if desired.

Makes 6 servings (about 5 cups)

Savory Chicken and Oregano Chili

3 cans (15 ounces each) Great Northern *or* cannellini beans, drained

3½ cups chicken broth

2 cups chopped cooked chicken

2 medium red bell peppers, cored, seeded and chopped

1 medium onion, peeled and chopped

1 can (4 ounces) diced green chiles

3 cloves garlic, minced

2 teaspoons ground cumin

1 teaspoon salt

1 tablespoon minced fresh oregano

1. Place beans, broth, chicken, bell peppers, onion, chiles, garlic, cumin and salt in **CROCK-POT®** slow cooker. Mix well to combine. Cover; cook on LOW 8 to 10 hours or on HIGH 4 to 5 hours.

2. Stir in oregano before serving.

Makes 8 servings

Simmering Hot and Sour Soup

2 cans (14½ ounces each) chicken broth

1 cup chopped cooked chicken *or* pork

4 ounces fresh shiitake mushroom caps, thinly sliced

½ cup thinly sliced bamboo shoots

3 tablespoons rice wine vinegar

2 tablespoons soy sauce

1½ teaspoons chili paste *or* 1 teaspoon hot chili oil

4 ounces firm tofu, well drained and cut into ½-inch pieces

2 teaspoons sesame oil

2 tablespoons cornstarch

2 tablespoons cold water

Chopped cilantro or sliced green onions

1. Combine broth, chicken, mushrooms, bamboo shoots, vinegar, soy sauce and chili paste in **CROCK-POT**® slow cooker. Cover; cook on LOW 3 to 4 hours or on HIGH 2 to 3 hours or until chicken is cooked through.

2. Stir in tofu and sesame oil. Combine cornstarch with water; mix well. Add to soup and mix in well. Cover; cook on HIGH 10 minutes or until soup has thickened. To serve, sprinkle with cilantro.

Makes 4 servings

INDEX

INDEX

INDEX

INDEX

INDEX

INDEX

METRIC CHART

VOLUME MEASUREMENTS (dry)

$\frac{1}{8}$ teaspoon = 0.5 mL
$\frac{1}{4}$ teaspoon = 1 mL
$\frac{1}{2}$ teaspoon = 2 mL
$\frac{3}{4}$ teaspoon = 4 mL
1 teaspoon = 5 mL
1 tablespoon = 15 mL
2 tablespoons = 30 mL
$\frac{1}{4}$ cup = 60 mL
$\frac{1}{3}$ cup = 75 mL
$\frac{1}{2}$ cup = 125 mL
$\frac{2}{3}$ cup = 150 mL
$\frac{3}{4}$ cup = 175 mL
1 cup = 250 mL
2 cups = 1 pint = 500 mL
3 cups = 750 mL
4 cups = 1 quart = 1 L

VOLUME MEASUREMENTS (fluid)

1 fluid ounce (2 tablespoons) = 30 mL
4 fluid ounces ($\frac{1}{2}$ cup) = 125 mL
8 fluid ounces (1 cup) = 250 mL
12 fluid ounces ($1\frac{1}{2}$ cups) = 375 mL
16 fluid ounces (2 cups) = 500 mL

WEIGHTS (mass)

$\frac{1}{2}$ ounce = 15 g
1 ounce = 30 g
3 ounces = 90 g
4 ounces = 120 g
8 ounces = 225 g
10 ounces = 285 g
12 ounces = 360 g
16 ounces = 1 pound = 450 g

DIMENSIONS

$\frac{1}{16}$ inch = 2 mm
$\frac{1}{8}$ inch = 3 mm
$\frac{1}{4}$ inch = 6 mm
$\frac{1}{2}$ inch = 1.5 cm
$\frac{3}{4}$ inch = 2 cm
1 inch = 2.5 cm

OVEN TEMPERATURES

250°F = 120°C
275°F = 140°C
300°F = 150°C
325°F = 160°C
350°F = 180°C
375°F = 190°C
400°F = 200°C
425°F = 220°C
450°F = 230°C

BAKING PAN AND DISH EQUIVALENTS

Utensil	Size in Inches	Size in Centimeters	Volume	Metric Volume
Baking or Cake Pan (square or rectangular)	8×8×2	20×20×5	8 cups	2 L
	9×9×2	23×23×5	10 cups	2.5 L
	13×9×2	33×23×5	12 cups	3 L
Loaf Pan	8½×4½×2½	21×11×6	6 cups	1.5 L
	9×9×3	23×13×7	8 cups	2 L
Round Layer Cake Pan	8×1½	20×4	4 cups	1 L
	9×1½	23×4	5 cups	1.25 L
Pie Plate	8×1½	20×4	4 cups	1 L
	9×1½	23×4	5 cups	1.25 L
Baking Dish or Casserole			1 quart/4 cups	1 L
			1½ quart/6 cups	1.5 L
			2 quart/8 cups	2 L
			3 quart/12 cups	3 L